How To Create a Microsoft Edge Extension (And Sell it!)

By Daniel Melehi

©2025 Edition

Contents

Introduction

Welcome to *How To Create a Microsoft Edge Extension (And Sell it!)*. I'm thrilled you've decided to embark on this journey with me. As I look back on my own adventure in creating browser extensions, I recall the excitement, the late-night coding sessions, and the exhilaration of seeing my work listed in an official add-ons store. In this book, I want to bring you along for every step of that process—everything from the initial spark of an idea to the triumphant moment of sharing your finished extension with the world.

I still remember the first time I realized there was a whole realm of possibilities lurking beneath the hood of a web browser. I noticed tiny add-on icons perched on the toolbar, each offering some specialized function. It dawned on me: these little pieces of software had the power to change the way we experience the internet. At that moment, I decided to become a creator rather than merely a user. This shift in perspective led me down a path that would eventually result in my first extension—an intuitive tool that streamlined my daily tasks.

The beauty of building an extension for Microsoft Edge lies in its fluid ecosystem. The modern Edge browser is built on the Chromium project, which means there's a welcoming environment filled with readily available APIs and well-documented materials. As you learn the ropes, you'll discover that coding for Edge extensions is both rewarding and less intimidating than you might expect. You don't need an enormous team or a pile of expensive hardware. All you truly need is your determination, a reliable computer, and a willingness to tinker until something remarkable emerges.

Throughout this book, I'll share my personal stories—both the breakthroughs and the mistakes I've made—and hopefully, these anecdotes will guide you beyond the obstacles I encountered. We'll begin with an overview of what extensions are and why they matter. Next, we'll plan out your very own project, considering your goals, the scope of your audience, and the features necessary to make your extension stand out. After that, we'll step into the nuts and bolts of setting up your development environment, exploring the essential technologies that form an extension's foundation.

Then we'll navigate the core architecture that underpins every browser extension. You'll see just how these components—like background scripts, content scripts, and the manifest file—come together to create a seamless user experience. Trust me, once you see this architecture in action, you'll find it easier to mold a new feature or fix an unwieldy bug because you'll understand exactly how everything fits together.

One crucial piece of wisdom I learned the hard way is the importance of planning: from the very start, you should have a solid blueprint. Yes, spontaneous creativity is powerful, but a stable roadmap ensures you won't waste time wandering down dead-end paths. With a plan in hand, we'll delve into the specifics of implementing features, ensuring your extension offers genuine solutions and stands out in a crowded marketplace.

In the later sections of this book, we'll dive into testing, packaging, and publishing your work for others to use. Of course, the story doesn't end at launch. You'll also explore how to market and potentially monetize your extension, providing you with a chance to earn some extra income—or even build a thriving business— around your passion for development.

Beyond that, we'll delve into advanced techniques like integrating third-party services, enhancing security, expanding cross-browser compatibility, and evolving your extension in response to user feedback. In short, you'll see how to refine and grow your extension so it never becomes stagnant, ensuring you stay relevant in an ever-moving digital landscape.

So, welcome aboard! By the end of this book, you'll have the blueprint, skill set, and inspiration you need to bring your own Microsoft Edge extension to life, and yes, to **sell it** if that's part of your grand plan. My hope is that my story, experiences, and insights will not only give you a strong technical foundation but also encourage you to take bold creative leaps. Let's get started and see just how far your extension can go.

Chapter 1: Understanding the Basics of Extensions

When I first began exploring browser extensions, I was instantly captivated by their ability to customize and enhance my web experience. I remember feeling like I'd uncovered a secret portal that let me bend the browser to my will—adding buttons, altering webpages, and automating repetitive tasks. The concept might sound simple, but the more I dove in, the more I realized that these small add-ons could hold a profound impact on productivity and entertainment alike.

Extensions, at their core, are software components that extend or modify the browser's functionality. They can do everything from blocking ads and generating secure passwords to translating languages and tracking package deliveries. In fact, the variety is practically limitless. Since Microsoft Edge is built on Chromium, many extensions designed for similar platforms can be adapted to work in Edge with minimal changes, and vice versa. This level of flexibility is why I consider Edge extension development such a worthwhile skill to pursue.

In this first chapter, I want to paint a clear picture of what an extension is and why it's worth building one. Think of a browser extension as a set of small programs and configuration files packaged together. The hallmark file that unites these components is called a **manifest**, which outlines the rules, permissions, and resources that form the extension. If you envision your extension as a puzzle, the manifest is the box's cover that shows you how the final image should appear.

Behind the scenes, an extension typically includes **background scripts**, which run quietly in the background to handle tasks like event listening, data processing, and other behind-the-scenes work. You might also have **content scripts** that interact directly with web pages—accessing and modifying elements on the page. Additionally, **browser action** or **page action** scripts govern how your extension's button or icon responds to clicks and other browser interactions.

When I was learning these concepts, I found it helpful to group them into two main categories: the "front-end" part that users see and click, and the "back-end" portion that does the heavy lifting. Understanding these roles is essential because it influences how you structure your files, manage data flow, and even choose your programming architecture. For instance, if you need to store user preferences, you might lean heavily on the extension's storage APIs. If you plan to manipulate a webpage's interface, you'll rely more on content scripts and a deeper knowledge of DOM (Document Object Model) manipulation.

Over time, you'll discover that building a successful extension is partly about knowing which APIs to tap into and partly about delivering a clear benefit to your audience. The truly memorable extensions I've seen solve real problems—like quickly toggling a dark mode on websites or generating personalized text snippets for emails. They solve pain points in a way that's easy to understand and even fun to use.

From a broader perspective, browser extensions fall under the grand umbrella of web development. You'll see familiar technologies like HTML, CSS, and JavaScript. However, the key difference lies in how the browser interprets your code and the restricted environment in which extensions live. For security reasons, extensions must declare permissions they need—such as reading data on specific sites or interacting with tabs. These permissions are vital for transparency and, from my own experience, greatly affect user trust. After all, if an extension is requesting access to everything under the sun, users will naturally be skeptical.

In the pages ahead, we'll be dispelling the anxiety that can accompany learning new technologies. Just keep in mind the foundation you've gained here: an extension is a collection of scripts, styles, and resources, all unified by the manifest file. By clarifying these core building blocks, you'll find it much simpler to map out your own project and bring your ideas to life.

Now that we've acquainted ourselves with the fundamental structure and purpose of browser extensions, it's time to dive deeper. Next, we'll plan the extension you've been envisioning. Let's transform that fleeting idea into something tangible and remarkable.

Chapter 2: Planning Your Microsoft Edge Extension

Before diving headfirst into coding, I like to take a step back and lay out a plan, almost like drawing up a travel itinerary for a big adventure. When I built my very first extension, I rushed into coding right away—only to realize later that I was missing a cohesive strategy. It felt like assembling a jigsaw puzzle without looking at the picture on the box. Taking the time to strategize helped me keep my goals in focus and avoid a lot of frustration.

The planning phase starts with one crucial question: **What problem are you trying to solve?** Maybe you're tired of manually managing open tabs, or perhaps you need a quick tool that taps into an online service to fetch stock prices. Whatever the idea, make sure your extension offers a clear and concrete benefit. One method I've found helpful is writing a simple statement: "This extension will help users X by doing Y." This one-liner forces you to clarify your objective and keeps you focused on the essential purpose behind your creation.

Next, you'll want to define the **audience**. Are you developing this extension for professionals in a certain field, casual internet users, or a niche hobbyist group? Understanding your target user base influences the extension's design and features, and also guides you in how you'll market your final product. For example, when I created an extension to manage code snippets, I knew my target audience was fellow developers. This insight guided everything from my user interface to my extension's color scheme.

Part of planning also means determining your extension's **scope**. Because it's easy to get carried away with tons of features, I like to start small and ensure the core functionality is rock-solid. Then I note down any extra features as future enhancements. That approach keeps me from feeling overwhelmed and allows me to deliver a polished product early. People will appreciate your clarity of vision more than a jumble of half-completed features.

Once your idea takes shape, consider mapping out how the user will interact with the extension. Think about the user's journey: they install the extension, see an icon in their browser, click it, and access certain functionalities. It's almost like writing a little story about your user's experience. I often draw a simple flowchart: Start → Click Extension Icon → Perform Action → See Results. Then I expand each element with notes on how I plan to handle those actions in code. This approach serves as a mental "sneak peek" of how your extension will actually feel when it's put to use.

Another crucial part of your plan should be **research**. Check if there are similar extensions out there and identify what sets yours apart. It's not about avoiding competition; it's about delivering something uniquely valuable or improving on what others have done. Viewing existing solutions might also spark new ideas or highlight pitfalls to avoid. If you stumble upon a big competitor, it might mean the market is already validated and there's a demand for this type of extension.

As trivial as it might seem, I also recommend deciding on a name early on. A catchy, descriptive name has a powerful way of forming your brand identity. It doesn't have to be final—some of my projects changed names multiple times—but having a placeholder name plants a flag in your mind. It's like naming a character in a novel; they begin to feel real once they have a name.

Finally, give some thought to **technical constraints**. What languages and tools are you comfortable with? Do you plan to use any frameworks or libraries for more advanced features? The benefit of modern browser extension development is that you can rely on familiar web technologies. If you're proficient in JavaScript, let that skill carry you forward. However, plan for extra time if you decide to integrate complex APIs or try out a new framework you're less familiar with.

By considering all these factors—purpose, audience, scope, user journey, research, and technical constraints—you'll assemble a solid blueprint for your extension. Trust me, this blueprint will make the coding process less chaotic and leave you more time to refine what truly matters: crafting a tool that resonates with your audience. Ready to get your hands dirty? Let's move on to setting up your development environment so we can build out the vision you've been putting together.

Chapter 3: Setting Up Your Development Environment

I remember the first version of my development "environment": a random folder on my desktop labeled "test," where I threw HTML and JavaScript files. It might have worked briefly, but it was easy to get lost. Over time, I've learned that a well-structured setup can save you infinite headaches down the line. In this chapter, we'll get you organized so you can work efficiently and keep your extension's code neat and maintainable.

The best part is you don't need anything too fancy for Microsoft Edge extension development. First, you'll want to install **Microsoft Edge**—preferably the latest version—so you can test your work in a real browser environment. Next, you'll want a robust **code editor** like Visual Studio Code, Sublime Text, or any editor you're comfortable with that offers features like syntax highlighting and file organization.

With your tools in place, create a dedicated folder for your project. In my experience, naming that folder after the extension's working title helps keep your mind clear. Inside that folder, I typically create these subdirectories:

Folder Name	Purpose
css	Holds all external style sheets
js	Contains JavaScript files (background scripts, content scripts, etc.)
images	Stores icons, logos, or any graphic assets
_locales	Reserved for localization files if you plan to support multiple languages

Aside from these folders, you'll have the **manifest.json** file in the root of your project. The manifest file is the cornerstone of your extension's environment—defining permissions, names, icons, and references to the scripts and pages that compose your extension. We'll talk more about the manifest in a later chapter, but for now, just know that you'll need it as soon as you start testing.

Once you have a preliminary folder structure, you can load your in-progress extension in Edge without publishing it to the store. To do this, open the browser and head to *edge://extensions*. Switch on the **Developer Mode** toggle, then select **Load unpacked**. Choose the folder where you've placed your manifest.json file. If everything is set up correctly, your extension should appear in the list, sporting whatever name you assigned in the manifest.

Working with **version control** is another aspect of a well-organized environment. If you haven't already, install Git or use a version control tool that suits your workflow. I can't emphasize enough how vital this has been in my own projects. Whenever I experiment with a new feature, I branch out in Git. This way, if I end up down a dead-end path, I can roll back easily without fear. Plus, it provides a historical record of your project's progress, which is invaluable for debugging or revisiting old ideas.

In addition, consider establishing a simple build process if your extension grows to be more complex. Tools like Webpack, Rollup, or Gulp can help bundle and minify your scripts. While not required for smaller extensions, these tools keep large-scale projects manageable. If you're inserting advanced features— like React or Angular for the extension's front-end— these bundlers become even more essential.

A trick I've adopted is creating a short **README** file inside the project folder, even if it's just for my eyes. In it, I note the commands for building or loading the extension, as well as any environment variables I might need. This file doubles as quick documentation for anyone else who might collaborate on the project in the future—or for "future me" when I've forgotten the details of my own setup.

Once your environment is in place, you're positioned to start bringing your extension's functionality to life. It's a system where you understand exactly where each piece belongs and how it all interacts. It's like having a tidy toolbox—you don't have to sift through a jumbled mess to find the right wrench. By investing a little time now, you'll be able to iterate rapidly and experiment freely without losing track of your progress.

With your foundation now set, we're going to roll up our sleeves and delve into the **Core Extension Architecture** in the next chapter. That's where we dive deeper into background scripts, content scripts, and how they communicate. Exciting times are ahead as we build upon the environment you've just established!

Chapter 4: Core Extension Architecture

When I was piecing together my first extension, I likened the experience to constructing a small house. You have your blueprint (the manifest), you know what rooms you want (the functionality), and now you need to decide how those rooms connect and interact with each other. That's where understanding the Core Extension Architecture comes in. By the end of this chapter, you'll grasp how your background scripts, content scripts, and user interfaces harmonize to form a cohesive, functional extension.

Let's start with the **background script**. Think of it as the brain of your extension, always running behind the scenes—though often in a dormant state, awakening when events occur. Common examples of events might be when a user opens a new tab or clicks a button in your extension. If you're building an application that listens for real-time updates or fetches data periodically, the background script is your go-to. One of my early projects involved tracking cryptocurrency prices, and I used the background script to ping an API every few minutes and then update the extension's badge with the latest prices.

On the other end, you have **content scripts**, which embed themselves into web pages. Imagine they're like guests who enter the room of a webpage and can rearrange the furniture. They can read, modify, or enhance the page's content. A prime example would be an ad blocker that scans the DOM to find and hide ad elements. Or a language translator that identifies text and swaps it out with translations. Remember, content scripts exist within the context of the webpage, so they have to play by the webpage's DOM rules.

But how do these two parts communicate with each other? They do so through **message passing**. Think of it like an old-fashioned tube system in large corporate buildings: the content script can send a message up the tube to the background script, and the background script can respond or send its own messages back. This system helps maintain a separation of concerns. If you have an analytics function in the background but you need the user's current webpage data, the content script can gather that data and then send it to the background script for processing.

Alongside background scripts and content scripts, there's often a **browser action** or **popup** page. When you click on the extension icon, a small window can appear, showcasing a user interface—buttons, forms, or real-time data. This interface is essentially a mini web page made up of HTML, CSS, and JavaScript. It's a good place for users to trigger actions or adjust settings. For instance, if I had a note-taking extension, I'd let users type in that popup, save the note, and then the background script would store it.

The architecture becomes even more interesting when you include **options pages**. These are settings pages where users can customize the extension's behavior, like choosing a theme color or specifying advanced preferences. Options pages are typically opened from a link in the extension's management screen or via the popup. Having an options page is a neat way to keep the popup uncluttered while also providing advanced configurations for power users.

One common pitfall is trying to do all the work inside a single script. Believe me, I tried that once. It quickly became a tangled web of data passes, with the content script trying to store data and the background script trying to manipulate the DOM. This approach is bound to become unwieldy. Keeping responsibilities separated not only helps with clarity but also makes debugging far easier. When something breaks, you can zero in on the specific script responsible for that piece of functionality.

Now, let's talk about **permissions** very briefly. Each extension must declare the permissions it needs in the manifest, such as "tabs" or "activeTab." This is part of your architecture because it determines how your background scripts and content scripts can operate. If you're dealing with multiple domains or certain browser APIs, you'll need to declare them. It's not just a bureaucratic requirement; it also informs users about your extension's capabilities and fosters trust.

In practice, your extension might look like this: A background script waits for a "browser action clicked" event. Once clicked, a popup appears where the user enters information. The popup's script then sends the data to the background. If the user is on a specific website, the background script may ask the content script to modify certain elements. This interplay between background, content, and possibly an options page, all under the umbrella of declared permissions, forms the spine of a well-structured extension.

By consciously designing your extension's architecture, you'll ensure that each part of your code has a distinct role. It's a bit like a well-coordinated team: the background script handles the heavy lifting and event management, content scripts interact directly with web pages, and your popup or options page let users control settings without ever leaving the browser. This structure keeps the extension efficient, maintainable, and—dare I say—fun to work on.

Now that you have a solid understanding of these architectural components, you're ready to dive deeper into the actual implementation and the crucial details— like writing your manifest file and making full use of Microsoft Edge's APIs. Believe me, this foundational knowledge will illuminate everything you do going forward, making the process smoother and even more rewarding.

Chapter 5: Crafting the Manifest File

The very first time I laid eyes on a manifest file, I felt like I was peering into an extension's DNA. It's incredible how this single JSON document orchestrates every aspect of what your extension can do. From telling the browser which scripts to load to specifying how the extension interacts with user data, the manifest is your main point of reference. Over the years, I've grown to appreciate how an organized and well-structured manifest can make or break the success of your entire project.

I like to think of the manifest file as a backstage pass. It grants you, as the developer, official permission to ask the browser for certain capabilities, declare which pages you want to interact with, and define how you want the extension to display its icon. This sense of control is both empowering and humbling. On one hand, you get the freedom to shape the entire user experience. On the other, you need to remain responsible and respect the user's trust by only requesting the privileges you truly need.

When you're structuring the manifest file, the **name** of your extension acts as its identity. I remember agonizing over the name for one of my earliest projects, wanting it to sound memorable yet informative. Next, the **version** field is equally important, since it indicates how your extension evolves. Every update—whether it's a big new feature or a small bug fix—should come with a version increment. It's a practice that pays off when users start appreciating those incremental improvements.

Then there's the **description** field. In my experience, a concise and persuasive description in your manifest can play a huge role in generating curiosity. Sometimes, this text is displayed on the extension details page in the add-ons store, so I like to pack as much clarity and excitement into it as possible. Users will glance at this short snippet before deciding whether your tool is worth a try, so it's essential to craft it in a way that resonates with their needs.

One of the first real breakthroughs for me came when I fully understood how to link the **background** script using the manifest. By declaring a background service worker or a script, I allowed the browser to keep an ear out for specific events, even when no interface was visible. That was a game-changer—knowing, for instance, that my extension could track changes on a website in the background and then alert the user whenever something important happened. This behind-the-scenes functionality is at the heart of what makes extensions so powerful.

On top of that, the manifest lets you define **content scripts**—the scripts that run in the context of the webpages you visit. I still remember how excited I was when I realized I could add a content script block in the manifest that included a list of URLs I wanted to target. Whenever I visited those pages, my custom JavaScript would inject itself, seamlessly altering the webpage in ways that felt almost magical. This interplay between the background script and content scripts is carefully managed through the definitions in the manifest.

Furthermore, specifying the **icons** is another critical task in the manifest. Icons give your extension a visual identity, so choosing them wisely can help it stand out. I once spent days tweaking pixels to ensure the icon looked neat in both light and dark browser themes. Finally, permission declarations go hand in hand with everything else. Listing only the permissions you need ensures that users feel secure installing your extension. If the list looks too extensive, they might hit the

"Cancel" button out of concern. Keeping it lean with a transparent explanation is key to forming a strong bond of trust.

All in all, the manifest file is like the root of a grand family tree. Each branch—be it a script, an icon, or a permission—must be accounted for in this master document. Whenever I revisit my manifest, I feel like I'm peering back into the blueprint of my project's entire purpose. It's both comforting and invigorating to know that by editing a single file, I can reshape the extension's capabilities. This power, once understood, opens the door for countless innovative features that help users surf the web in more imaginative ways.

Chapter 6: Leveraging the Microsoft Edge APIs

When I first discovered how expansive Microsoft Edge's APIs could be, it felt like unlocking an entirely new level in a favorite video game. Suddenly, I wasn't just building an extension—I was building an interactive piece of software that could communicate with the browser in fascinating ways. From handling tabs and windows to tapping into the bookmarks manager, each API showcased new possibilities for weaving my ideas directly into the user's browsing routine.

The beauty of these APIs lies in their versatility. Edge, built on Chromium, shares many of the same extension APIs used by other Chromium-based browsers, which means you have a large ecosystem of knowledge and documentation at your disposal. Yet, specific Edge features can also deliver unique advantages. I vividly recall the moment I realized I could sync data effortlessly across multiple Edge instances by integrating browser-specific storage APIs. This meant a user could hop from their home computer to their work laptop and maintain the exact same data in my extension—like having a personal butler who follows you from one room to the next.

One of my favorite forays into the Edge API landscape was with the **tabs** API. It let me manipulate open tabs: create them, navigate them, or even listen for changes. You might wonder why that's exciting, but once you see how beneficial it is to automate repetitive tab management tasks, you'll get it. For instance, I built a feature that searched for duplicated tabs, consolidating them into a single location. It felt like digital spring cleaning. Users thanked me for saving them from an ocean of tab clutter.

Then there's the **runtime** API, a personal favorite for enabling inter-script communication. If I needed my content script to whisper something to the background script, runtime messaging was the solution. Quite often, I'd set up tiny "mailboxes" where each script could send messages back and forth without confusion. This approach kept my code base organized, allowing each component to excel at its own job and collaborate only when necessary.

Speaking of collaboration, I found the **storage** API particularly empowering. Working in synergy with the runtime messaging system, storage can maintain user settings, session details, or saved data for offline analysis. In one of my earlier projects—an extension that tracked how much time I spent on certain websites—I used the storage API to hold daily logs. Every morning, I'd retrieve that log, update it in real time, and watch as the extension's popup displayed my stats for the day. That sense of seeing data come to life was incredibly motivating for me.

Over time, I also learned to integrate **bookmarks** and **history** APIs into more specialized projects. On one occasion, I aimed to create a reading manager that could group interesting articles together and remove outdated links. By tapping into the bookmarks API, my extension kept track of user-specified folders, neatly organizing articles based on categories. Meanwhile, the history API allowed me to monitor browsing frequency, so each user's recommended articles could be tailored to their preferences.

For security-minded developers, the **webRequest** API opens the door to analyzing and modifying network requests. I've used it to block certain ads and even rewrite headers when a site needed a tweak for testing purposes. However, I quickly realized that powerful APIs require a delicate approach. You must clearly state your intentions in the manifest, and you have to ensure you're handling user data responsibly. It reminds me of operating heavy machinery: incredibly helpful, but best used with the right precautions.

Ultimately, exploring Edge's APIs feels like rummaging through a treasured toolbox. Each function, method, and event handler offers a potential solution to a nagging problem or a springboard to an innovative feature. By designing your extension around these built-in capabilities, you not only empower yourself but also extend that empowerment to your users. They get to experience the browser in a way that's strikingly personal—shaped by your creative touch. And in that sense, leveraging the Microsoft Edge APIs is more than just coding; it's about crafting an experience that lingers in the user's digital life.

Chapter 7: Designing User-Friendly Interfaces

When I embarked on my first extension project, I naively believed that as long as the functionality worked, the user interface could be a second thought. It didn't take long to learn how glaringly wrong I was. Users want an interface that feels intuitive and looks appealing, especially since they're already dealing with a cluttered online environment. Over time, I came to treat interface design like a critical piece of the puzzle. After all, it's often that first impression that determines if someone adopts your tool or dismisses it within seconds.

One major insight struck me when I noticed how users interact with extensions: they typically engage in short bursts. They click the toolbar icon, glance at information or adjust a setting, and then move on. With that in mind, I started focusing on a clean, streamlined popup design. If you're building a weather extension, you want the current temperature and forecast to be right there, front and center—no extra clicks needed. Achieving that level of immediacy requires careful planning and a willingness to remove anything superfluous.

I've also found it helpful to treat the extension's **popup** as a starting point, not the entire interface. Occasionally, you'll need a full **options page** to house more advanced or less frequently accessed settings. For instance, in one of my note-taking extensions, the popup included quick-access buttons for creating or viewing notes, while the detailed preferences for syncing and color themes lived in the options page. This separation kept the popup interface decluttered, yet still allowed power users to dive deeper.

Color schemes and typography are subtler aspects of UI design that can still significantly affect how an extension feels. I once spent an entire weekend experimenting with different color palettes to find a combination that was both visually inviting and easy on the eyes. Simplifying color choices helped my extension blend seamlessly with Edge's default toolbar look. I noticed that users didn't feel jarred by a radically different aesthetic—an important consideration if you want your extension to feel like a natural extension of the browser.

Another point that profoundly impacted my approach is the need for responsive design. Even though an extension's popup seems like a tiny, fixed window, users might resize their browser or use various display settings. By adopting responsive web design principles—using flexible layouts and media queries— I ensured that my interface remained crisp and readable across different screen resolutions. Whenever I tested my UI, I'd lower my screen resolution, enlarge it to a high-definition monitor, and even tweak the browser's zoom levels to confirm everything still looked polished.

For interactive elements, such as buttons and input fields, it's essential to offer clear visual feedback. If a button doesn't offer any hover or click indication, users can get confused about whether their action registered. I love using subtle micro-animations—like a brief color shift or a slight bounce on click—to reassure them. Over time, I've discovered that these small interactions can elevate the perceived quality of an extension, even if the underlying functionalities remain the same.

Error states and loading indicators are equally important but often overlooked. When an API call is taking longer than expected, a simple spinner or progress bar can relieve user anxiety. Alternatively, if something goes wrong—like a missing permission—presenting a friendly and informative error message can turn a frustrating moment into a chance to educate. In one of my earliest extensions, I discovered that a kindly worded error message with a quick fix link drove better user satisfaction than a cryptic console log ever could.

Finally, don't underestimate the power of **user testing**. I used to think I knew exactly what my users wanted until I watched a friend navigate my extension. The simple act of watching their cursor hesitate or hearing them voice confusion taught me more than any analytics report could. People appreciate an extension that "just works," and designing it well from the outset can foster a positive relationship that keeps them coming back. With a thoughtful, user-friendly interface, you're not just offering a tool—you're delivering an experience that can brighten someone's day, if only for a moment.

Chapter 8: Managing Permissions and Security

Early in my extension-building journey, I noticed there was a fine line between creating a powerful tool and overstepping the user's sense of security. The manifest file lets you declare which browser permissions you need, but that doesn't automatically grant you user trust. If your extension requests sweeping access to every website, your potential audience might think twice before installing it. Over time, I learned the importance of balancing your extension's capabilities with respecting the privacy and comfort of the people using it.

One of the first things I do when designing an extension is list the exact permissions I'll need, nothing more and nothing less. If my tool requires reading a webpage's content, I tailor that permission to specific sites or contexts. This might mean using "activeTab" rather than "tabs," or restricting host permissions to a known domain. By narrowing down the scope, I reassure users that my extension isn't peering into every aspect of their browsing habits. Ultimately, clarity in your scope fosters a bond of trust.

I also found that straightforward documentation goes a long way. For instance, if I need to read user data from a web page, I'll include a short explanation in my extension's description or on my website. A friendly sentence like, "We only scan the URLs you currently visit to provide relevant suggestions, and we do not store that data anywhere else," can alleviate fears. People generally don't mind giving up certain permissions if they understand precisely why those permissions are required.

Beyond the manifest, you'll want to ensure that your code handles data securely. I remember stumbling upon a nasty bug in one of my earlier projects, where an internal variable storing authentication tokens was accidentally printed in the console. Technically, a user would have to dig pretty deep to find it, but it was still a vulnerability I had to fix fast. Now, whenever I'm working with sensitive data—like login credentials or API keys—I make an effort to encrypt or obfuscate what I can. If encryption isn't possible, I minimize data exposure by storing it in ephemeral memory rather than local storage.

Then there's the matter of external resources. Sometimes you'll want to pull in a JavaScript library or a CDN resource for convenience, but that can introduce risks if the external file is ever compromised. I remember reading horror stories about supply-chain attacks where once-trusted libraries were hijacked to inject malicious code. These cautionary tales led me to a stricter policy: I either self-host my scripts or use a service that verifies the integrity of those resources. By controlling my code pipeline, I shield both myself and my users from nasty surprises.

I'd also emphasize the role of constant updates. Security is never a one-and-done effort. Each time I push a new version, I take a moment to review whether any new features might inadvertently open a vulnerability. A quick internal audit can uncover unexpected behaviors, such as a new API call that logs too much user information. This process is much easier if you keep your extension's architecture modular and well-documented. Fixes can be rolled out faster, and you're less likely to break something else while plugging security gaps.

Of course, building user trust is about more than just technical measures. Sometimes, it's as simple as transparent communication. In one instance, I had to add an extra permission to read user bookmarks. Rather than slipping it into the manifest quietly, I published a changelog explaining exactly why I needed it. The response was surprisingly positive, and I learned that people are more than willing to accept changes if you treat them like partners in the process.

Managing permissions and security might seem like a tedious side of extension development, but I actually find it rewarding. By handling these aspects responsibly, I know I'm building something that respects people and their online boundaries. And when they install my extension without hesitation, that trust is a silent affirmation that all my careful planning was well worth the effort.

Chapter 9: Troubleshooting and Debugging

Back when I was new to extension development, I can recall entire afternoons spent scrolling through console logs in search of that elusive bug. Perhaps you've been there too—frustrated, eyes burning, determined to figure out why your code behaves differently than you intended. Over time, I've collected a handful of troubleshooting strategies that have saved my sanity more times than I can count. Each new project is like a puzzle, and these methods form the puzzle-solving toolkit that I reach for when something goes awry.

My first piece of advice? Make liberal use of **console logging**, but do it wisely. I've seen developers add console.log statements after practically every line of code, which creates a towering avalanche of messages that can be hard to interpret. Instead, I try to log only critical points—like when a user action triggers a significant function, or when an if-else branch decides a path. By marking up code with carefully chosen log statements, I can see the decision-making flow and identify precisely where an unexpected behavior sneaks in.

The built-in **Developer Tools** in Microsoft Edge deserve a round of applause, too. They provide insights into network requests, background scripts, and content scripts in real time. When debugging content scripts, I love that I can open the DevTools right on the website I'm interacting with and see how the scripts transform the page. Meanwhile, the dedicated extension debugging panel for background scripts is a blessing. It shows every console message, plus the state of local or sync storage.

I've also discovered that the **Edge extension menu** offers a quick path for reloading an extension after I make changes. There's a certain rhythm to the process: tweak code, save, reload extension, retest. Sometimes it feels repetitive, but it beats burying yourself in deeper troubleshooting while using an old build. If you forget to reload, you'll chase your tail fixing a problem that might've already been solved in your new code. I learned that lesson the hard way once, spending nearly an hour diagnosing an "issue" that was fixed ages ago.

When the issues grow more complex, I rely on **breakpoints** in the DevTools. Being able to pause the code mid-execution is like stopping time and searching for clues at the scene of the crime. I'll carefully inspect the values of variables, or analyze which function calls happened right before the breakpoint. It's a meticulous but satisfying process. Once I pinpoint the suspicious variable, I can fine-tune the logic around it.

For network-related issues—maybe an API call that's returning funny data—I head over to the **Network tab** in DevTools. I'll track the request to see the exact payload leaving my extension and the response that comes back. More than once, I've discovered that a minor typo in my request body was causing the server to send an odd response. Fixing that type of bug is quick once you spot it, but maddening if you're scouring your code without examining the actual request traffic.

Sometimes, problems don't just lie in the code but in the **manifest**. If I misspell a permission or forget to declare a key script, my extension might silently fail to load the relevant functionality. I recall one occasion where a long day of hair-pulling ended when I noticed I'd typed "contet_scripts" instead of "content_scripts." After that fiasco, I religiously double-check my manifest file whenever a new feature acts strangely.

Lastly, don't hesitate to lean on **community resources**. Forums, Q&A boards, and developer circles are brimming with folks who've wrestled with similar issues. Often the fix is a single line of code or a small tweak in your approach. I've learned that being humble enough to ask for help can expedite your progress exponentially. So, whether you're sifting through logs or stepping through breakpoints, remember that every bug you tackle refines both your extension and your skill set. It's all part of the journey, one step closer to an impeccably functioning piece of software that you can proudly share with the world.

Chapter 10: Testing and Quality Assurance

I still remember the sense of pride I felt the first time my extension ran without any apparent glitches—until a friend uncovered a bizarre bug that broke everything. That incident taught me the value of structured testing and thorough quality assurance. In my early days of development, I used to rely on my own click-through attempts as my main testing routine. But I soon realized that this ad hoc approach left plenty of blind spots. I needed a system that would systematically catch flaws before real users experienced them.

My testing journey began with an emphasis on **functional tests**. I made a list of every feature my extension claimed to offer. Then, I created mini-scenarios—for instance, if a user clicks the icon when they have multiple tabs open, the extension should display a particular message. I walked through each scenario step by step, compiling notes about what worked and what went wrong. Over time, I turned these scenarios into a structured checklist, which proved invaluable when I updated my code and needed a quick re-verification method.

One approach I adopted was to simulate a range of **user behaviors**, from the most obvious ones to the downright odd. For instance, I had a friend who always opened multiple browser windows and navigated away before my extension finished loading. Predictably, I discovered several timing-related bugs that cropped up when the extension tried to process data from a closed window. That experience showed me that real-world usage can be messy, and thorough testing has to reflect that chaos.

I also learned to respect the importance of **cross-environment tests**. Different operating systems, screen resolutions, or even network speeds can affect everything from layout alignment to how quickly a core function executes. I once assumed my extension would behave identically on a Mac and a Windows machine. Yet, a handful of UI elements shifted unexpectedly, causing layout overlaps in the Windows environment. A few user complaints later, I made cross-platform checks a permanent item on my quality checklist.

Beyond functional considerations, **performance testing** became a key aspect of my routine. I ran timing benchmarks to see how my extension performed under various conditions. If tasks took too long or hogged too much memory, I knew I risked frustrating my users. I once built a feature that parsed large blocks of text, and it worked flawlessly with small samples. But on massive documents, it bogged down. A quick stress test helped me identify the culprit and optimize my parsing logic before a wave of negative reviews could hit.

Automated tests came next in my process. Although not every scenario easily fits into an automated script, I started building small test suites using frameworks compatible with browser extensions. While I still do plenty of manual checking, these automated tests gave me peace of mind whenever I refactored code. Instead of posting updates and hoping for the best, I let these scripts confirm that core functionalities remained intact. That confidence boost alone was worth the effort of writing the tests.

Additionally, **UI-specific tests** saved me many headaches. Early on, I'd rely on visual inspection: I'd open the popup, click a few buttons, and declare everything good to go. But subtle CSS changes or different device pixel ratios could trigger odd quirks—some impossible to spot at a quick glance. Now, I keep screenshots of my UI in various states. If anything differs from those baseline snapshots, I know right away that a styling drift has crept in. It's amazing how a tiny design tweak can have big consequences if undetected.

Finally, I always circle back to **user feedback** as the ultimate test. No matter how many checklists and automated scripts I have, real people will try things I never imagined. Whenever a bug surfaces in user reports, I treat it like a gold mine of information. Each fix contributes to a sturdier, more reliable extension. Over time, I've come to see testing and QA not as annoying hurdles, but as essential stepping stones to delivering a product I can claim with pride truly works across countless situations.

Chapter 11: Packaging Your Extension for Release

As I prepared for my first official release, I likened the experience to getting all dressed up for a big event. I had spent countless hours refining features, fixing bugs, and polishing my user interface. Now, it was time to bundle all that effort into a neat package that I could share with a wider audience. Little did I know that a small oversight in packaging could send me scrambling just as I was about to hit that "publish" button.

When I talk about "packaging," I'm referring to the final arrangement of files, scripts, images, and configurations. It's the moment when everything has to be in its right place. My first step is usually to do a final pass through the directory structure I've been working with. I remove any unused assets and double-check that all icons are present in the correct sizes. I've learned the hard way that a missing icon size can prompt an immediate rejection from the add-ons store or cause an awkward user experience if the browser tries to display a non-existent image.

I then turn my attention to the **manifest** file. This is where little mistakes cause big headaches. If any new permissions or features were introduced late in development, I ensure those are properly declared. It's also important to confirm that I haven't accidentally requested permissions I decided not to use. If I see references to an API my extension no longer needs, I remove them. It's a balancing act: requesting too many permissions can raise eyebrows, but forgetting a vital one will break part of the functionality.

In addition, I pay close attention to my **version numbers**. I once forgot to increment the version before packaging, which caused confusion when the older extension tried to update itself incorrectly. Now, I follow a simple versioning system—major.minor.patch—and I make sure the manifest reflects the latest build. That overall consistency helps me keep track of which iteration is live, which is in testing, and which I should retire.

I still recall an instance when I nearly released a build containing my unminified, development-only scripts. A friend caught me just in time. While there's nothing inherently wrong with shipping readable code, I prefer bundling, minifying, or transpiling it when appropriate to improve performance and obfuscate sensitive logic. Additionally, minified code can sometimes save a few kilobytes, which might matter for users on slower connections or those with limited bandwidth.

Preparing a **change log** is also part of my packaging routine. Whether I'm introducing new functionalities or merely refining existing features, I note these changes so users understand what's new—and, if necessary, how to use it. Including a concise summary and a few bullet points can transform your extension updates from mysterious background events into informative milestones that keep users in the loop. And if you're anything like me, having a record of changes is helpful for your own memory too.

Before finalizing the package, I also run a final **performance check**. I ensure that nothing's suddenly hogging CPU cycles or freezing the browser. Sometimes, last-minute code tweaks have unintended consequences. Keeping a watchful eye on the performance metrics has saved me from releasing an extension that performs great in short tests but degrades over longer sessions. This final check can involve everything from verifying memory usage in the browser's Task Manager to simulating slower network conditions.

Once I'm confident in every part of my extension—its manifest, icons, scripts, and performance—I bundle it all up. Depending on my setup, I might generate a ZIP file or another compressed format that the add-ons store expects. I still get a flutter of excitement at this stage, knowing that everything is nearly ready for the public. Next stop: the wide world of publishing. And trust me, that's an adventure in its own right.

Chapter 12: Publishing on the Microsoft Edge Add-ons Store

Standing at the doorway of the Microsoft Edge Add-ons Store feels a bit like stepping onto a stage. There's a pinch of pride and a dash of anxiety, knowing folks all around the world will soon judge, download, and hopefully love what I've created. Yet no matter how many times I've published an extension, each new launch has its own set of twists and turns. Over time, I've developed a personal checklist to ensure I stay cool under pressure.

First off, **account registration** is the gateway. If you don't already have one, you'll need a Microsoft Partner Center account to submit your extension. While filling out the details, I try to provide consistent information—like my developer name, website, and contact email—so users can easily verify my credibility. If your brand differs from your personal name, ensure your username and the extension listing align, so prospective users aren't confused about who's behind the software.

Once logged into the dashboard, you'll head over to the **submission** process. This is where you upload your carefully packaged extension file. One crucial consideration is to craft a compelling **listing description**. This text is your elevator pitch for potential users browsing the store. Whenever I write one, I like to highlight the extension's main benefits in plain language—no technical jargon, no fluff. A user typically spends only a few seconds deciding whether to install, so clarity is everything.

Then comes the **privacy policy**. Users and Microsoft alike take data security seriously, and your extension listing requires at least a minimal statement of how you handle data. I typically mention what data my extension collects—if any—and for what purpose, plus a brief promise that I don't resell information to third parties. This transparency goes a long way toward calming potential fears, and it also meets store guidelines.

Don't forget to **attach screenshots** or a short demo video. A quick glance at a screenshot can convey what your extension does far better than a block of text might. I tend to highlight the extension in use: showing the popup window, the options page, or any unique visual elements. This visual preview acts like a storefront display, tempting users to step inside and try what you're offering. The more polished your images, the better your chances of capturing attention.

Submission forms typically ask for **categories** or tags so users can find your extension based on their interests. I usually select the categories that best align with my extension's core functionality. If it's an organizational tool, "Productivity" might be a good fit. If it deals with finances, "Shopping" or "Finance" could be relevant. These categories help your extension show up in curated listings and searches, effectively boosting its discoverability from day one.

After submission, the Microsoft Edge team reviews your extension for policy compliance. My advice is to stay patient. Reviews can sometimes take longer than expected if there's a surge of new submissions. Occasionally, you might get a rejection citing specific policy violations. I've been through it—once, an obscure library I used triggered a potential trademark issue. Fixing it was straightforward once I knew the root cause. If you get similar feedback, address the concerns quickly, and resubmit.

Finally, when your extension goes live, it's time for a celebration! Users can now find and install it directly from the store. However, you'll also want to keep an eye on **reviews** and ratings. Good reviews can catch more downloads, while negative ones might point to issues you never anticipated. Even so, constructive criticism helps you improve. By responding politely to user comments and updating your extension promptly, you'll build a reputation for reliability that lasts well beyond launch day.

Chapter 13: Marketing Essentials

When I first launched an extension, I assumed that listing it in the store was enough to attract a constant stream of users. Reality soon set me straight. Without an effective marketing plan, even the most remarkable tools can remain hidden gems. I realized that marketing isn't a salesy chore; it's an opportunity to share my hard work with people who can genuinely benefit from it. Over time, I've picked up a few strategies—some learned through trial and error, others gleaned from industry experts—that I now consider essential.

One of my initial tactics was **word-of-mouth promotion**. I shared the extension link with friends, colleagues, and social media connections. This might feel small-scale at first, but personal endorsements carry a lot of weight. If a developer friend of mine tweets about a valuable extension, I'm much more inclined to try it. While it won't automatically catapult you to viral status, it can generate a few early adopters who can then spread the word further.

Next, I explored **developer communities and forums**. Sharing in specialized circles—like a subreddit for Microsoft Edge enhancements or a community forum for web developers—can yield targeted interest. People in these spaces already appreciate browser extensions and know their value well. You just need to be transparent about your extension's mission. I learned not to spam these forums with repetitive posts. Instead, I'd introduce my tool once, explaining its features and politely asking for feedback, which often sparked productive discussions.

Another technique that has served me well is crafting a **dedicated landing page**. Though it sounds like extra work, a well-designed page can be a hub for your extension's story, features, and testimonials. For an earlier project, I built a simple one-page site with screenshots, user reviews, and a direct "Install Now" button. It gave me a link to share outside the store—on social media, in email newsletters, or even on my resume. People often appreciate landing on a page that clarifies the extension's purpose at a glance.

I also dabbled in **email marketing**, particularly after collecting a small mailing list of interested users. Whenever I released a major update, I'd send out an announcement highlighting the new features. I made sure to keep my emails light and visually engaging, including bullet points that summarized improvements. This direct channel proved effective at re-engaging people who might have forgotten they had my extension installed, reminding them why it's worth keeping (and sharing).

Collaborations can open doors you didn't know existed. Whether it's **co-authoring blog posts** with other developers or asking influencers to review and demonstrate your extension, partnerships can amplify your reach dramatically. I remember teaming up with a content creator who specialized in productivity tips. By featuring my extension in his weekly video, I gained a significant spike in downloads. Sharing audiences can be a win-win situation if both parties have aligned interests.

Nothing, however, beats the power of **user reviews**. A slew of positive comments in the Microsoft Edge Add-ons Store can sway hesitant visitors. I encourage users to leave honest feedback by adding a short note in my extension's settings page or popup, inviting them to share their thoughts. This approach offers a gentle reminder without being intrusive. Over time, genuine reviews create social proof that reinforces your extension's value far more effectively than any ad campaign could.

In the end, marketing is all about communication. You've built something you believe in, but you must make that belief visible and compelling to others. Whether it's a thoughtful landing page, a friendly forum post, or a collaboration with an influencer, every piece of outreach educates potential users on how your extension can improve their browsing experience. Embracing these efforts took me beyond simply existing in the store to truly thriving there—and I'm confident it can do the same for you.

Chapter 14: Monetization and Revenue Models

I can trace my interest in monetizing extensions back to a day when I realized how much time and skill it took to keep my browser tools running smoothly. At the same time, I recognized that some users are more than willing to pay for valuable features or convenience. But I also worried about striking the right balance: how to generate a fair return without alienating the community that helped my extension flourish. Over time, I experimented with various models and discovered that monetization can be as creative as the development process itself.

One of my first attempts was a straightforward **donation button**. I put a small link in my extension's popup and on the landing page, inviting satisfied users to contribute any amount they felt comfortable with. While some folks were grateful enough to donate, this method alone didn't provide a consistent income. Still, it was a gentle way to dip my toes into monetization. It also helped me gauge user support without introducing paywalls or special tiers.

Later, I tried integrating **ads** into one of my projects. This choice required caution because browser extension users can be particularly sensitive to intrusive advertising. My approach was to display small, tasteful ads within a secondary panel of the extension—never interfering with the main functionality. Despite handling them thoughtfully, user feedback was mixed. Some appreciated the free tool and accepted the ads as compensation, while others found them distracting. Ultimately, I learned that advertising revenue could be viable, but only if executed with utmost respect for the user experience.

Another model that intrigued me was offering a **premium tier**. Imagine a free version with essential features and a paid upgrade for power users seeking more advanced capabilities. In one of my note-taking extensions, the premium version included collaborative editing, extra storage, and priority customer support. I discovered a loyal user base willing to pay monthly for these extras. The trick was ensuring the free version remained genuinely useful and didn't feel like a stripped-down demo. This balance often translates into a larger overall audience and a dedicated subset of paying customers.

Initially, I felt apprehensive about the **subscription model**. But monthly or yearly renewals can provide a stable income stream, which is especially appealing if you plan to keep updating your extension with fresh content or new features. Subscriptions also made me feel more accountable. If users were paying every month, I wanted to deliver consistent value—like new integrations or timely bug fixes. In many ways, the subscription model nudged me toward a more disciplined development approach.

In-app **purchase tokens** also found their way into my strategy. Picture an extension that offers a suite of downloadable templates or themes. Users can opt to buy only the assets they want, providing flexibility and avoiding a fixed monthly fee. This model caters to people who prefer one-time purchases over ongoing payments. I appreciate its incremental nature: small transactions can add up, and the user feels in control, no long-term commitment required.

Regardless of the revenue model, I eventually learned that **transparency** is the cornerstone of user trust. If you plan to collect data for targeted ads or if certain features are locked behind a paywall, spell it out clearly in your descriptions and user documentation. Bonus tip: a well-defined pricing structure sets the right expectations. When potential customers know exactly what they're getting—and how much it costs—they're less likely to be frustrated or leave negative reviews.

In the end, monetizing your extension isn't simply about turning a profit; it's about offering enough value that users see paying as a fair exchange for the benefits they gain. Whether you pick donations, ads, premium tiers, or something entirely different, ensure you keep the user experience front and center. That philosophy, in my experience, elevates both your tool and your relationship with the people who help support its ongoing development.

Chapter 15: Advanced Extension Functionality

I'll never forget the first time I pushed my extension beyond its basic scope. Sure, having a popup, background scripts, and content scripts felt solid, but I realized there was so much more potential under the hood. In this chapter, we'll explore how to unlock truly advanced features—those special tricks that make users pause and think, "Wow, that's handy." From persistent data storage to custom context menus, advanced functionality isn't just bells and whistles; it can transform your extension into a go-to solution users will swear by.

One of the first advanced features I encountered was **context menu integration**. Imagine a neat little right-click menu item that appears on specific elements of a webpage. From text selections to images, these custom menu entries let your users perform actions without leaving the site. I've created context menu features that trigger language translation, quick text formatting, and even snippet saving straight to a database. In my experience, it's the ultimate blend of convenience and seamlessness—turning an everyday right-click into a gateway to all sorts of extended capabilities.

Another huge leap for me was adding **persistent data storage**. I remember when I decided to store large sets of user preferences and logs. Local or sync storage

APIs suffice for smaller tasks, but if I needed to handle data that spanned multiple domains or sessions, I'd sometimes bring in IndexedDB for a more robust solution. Whether logging user activity, saving custom settings for each site, or caching data from third-party APIs, these advanced storage mechanisms opened up new horizons. By carefully structuring where and how data gets stored, you can keep performance snappy and ensure nothing gets lost when a user restarts their browser.

For those working on collaborative or real-time features, **communication channels** like WebSockets or the browser's native messaging pipeline can be a game-changer. I've built extensions that let teams co-edit shared notes, complete with indicators showing who's typing. Each user's changes ping out in near-real time, transforming the humble extension into a lightweight collaborative platform. The complexity can be daunting—balancing server-side code, user authentication, and data synchronization—but the payoff is a uniquely interactive experience that feels downright futuristic.

Then there's the realm of **DevTools integration**. You can create custom panels or sidebar pages in the Edge DevTools, letting fellow developers debug, analyze, or modify code seamlessly. I tried this approach for a project that analyzed webpage elements for SEO compliance. The custom DevTools panel highlighted meta tags and headers, notifying me of any that might be missing. If your user base includes tech-savvy folks, a well-crafted DevTools add-in can feel like a behind-the-scenes superpower. And for you as the creator, it's a chance to demonstrate a mastery of the intricate internal workings of the browser.

One advanced feature that caught my imagination was **automation and scripting**. With the right permissions, you could let users run mini-scripts or macros that automate repetitive tasks on web pages. I've seen people use this concept to auto-fill forms, parse data, or even apply styling changes to sites. However, caution is critical: you're treading a fine line between helpful automation and unexpectedly breaking a site's functionality. Thorough testing and clear user guidance have always been my compass whenever I veered into automation territory.

In my view, advanced functionality is about more than just adding sparkle—it's about elevating everyday workflows. Simplicity and elegance still matter, even when you're introducing high-level features. If I can seamlessly weave context menus, persistent data, custom DevTools panels, and automation into an extension without confusing or overwhelming the user, I know I've achieved something special. Many times, these are the features that separate a good extension from a truly indispensable one. As you dive into these advanced capabilities, keep an open mind and experiment freely. You never know which ambitious idea might become the key selling point that sets your extension apart in a crowded field.

Chapter 16: Integrating Third-Party Services

I distinctly remember the day I thought, "If only my extension could talk to that external service." It's one thing to build a tool that lives entirely within the browser, but hooking it into external APIs can expand its reach by leaps and bounds. From retrieving weather forecasts to processing payments, third-party integrations let you tap into specialized functionalities without reinventing the wheel. But like most powerful capabilities, it comes with nuances that can make or break the user experience—and the trust they place in you.

The first crucial step is choosing the **right service** to integrate with. I often start by listing what my extension can't do on its own. Maybe I want a translation engine, a backend database, or a real-time analytics dashboard. Once that's clear, I'll scour popular APIs to find a reliable partner. Reputation and stability are major concerns—if the external service crashes frequently or imposes harsh usage limits, it'll reflect poorly on my extension. In one project, I chose a free tier translation API only to find it limited daily requests to a tiny number, frustrating my users to no end.

Establishing **authentication** is typically the next big hurdle. Some APIs offer public endpoints, while others require OAuth or API tokens. I remember grappling with my first OAuth integration, trying to store refresh tokens securely and ensuring I didn't accidentally expose them to unscrupulous scripts. It was a lesson in balancing convenience (like saving tokens for immediate reuse) against security best practices (such as encrypting them or minimizing their time stored). My rule of thumb is to ask users for only what's strictly necessary to connect to the service; anything extra just opens doors to potential mishaps.

Once authentication is set, **request handling** becomes pivotal. I've learned to structure my code so that all external requests funnel through a dedicated module. This approach pays off when debugging. If something goes wrong—like a 401 error or a misquoted JSON property—I can pinpoint it quickly within that module instead of sifting through scattered scripts. Plus, if the third-party API changes its endpoints or format, I only need to tweak one place in my code rather than rummage through every function call.

Because you're pulling data from beyond the browser, **performance and reliability** come into play. For instance, if your extension depends on a weather service that sometimes lags, do you let users stare at a loading spinner? Or do you cache the last known forecast to show immediately, followed by an update once new data arrives? In my experience, gracefully handling such hiccups shows your audience you care about their time. A well-designed fallback mechanism can prevent your extension from feeling broken if the third-party service falters.

Next, there's the matter of making sense of the **incoming data**. Many external APIs deliver JSON payloads that might be chock-full of details your extension barely needs. Filtering or parsing that data on the fly helps keep things tidy. I once integrated a flight-tracking API that returned dozens of fields—plane altitudes, gate numbers, seat maps—when all I really needed was flight status and arrival time. Stripping out the noise not only sped up my extension but also simplified my code.

Finally, I can't overstate the importance of **clear user communication**. The data or functionality you retrieve from a third-party service is outside your direct control. If a feature relies on that service, I like to add a small note or symbol indicating it's powered by another platform. It's been my experience that this honesty fosters confidence—users appreciate knowing that if something acts up, it might be due to an external factor. Integrating third-party services can absolutely elevate your extension to new heights, but the key is meticulous planning and thoughtful implementation. When done correctly, your creation becomes more versatile and valuable, opening up possibilities you might never have imagined when you first started coding.

Chapter 17: Maintaining Security Best Practices

Early in my development journey, I learned a tough lesson: no matter how cool your extension is, one security slip-up can tarnish its reputation forever. I remember an incident where a user reported a minor data exposure in my code logs. Thankfully, it was just a small oversight—but it really drove home the importance of vigilance in securing every aspect of your extension. Whether you're handling user credentials, personal data, or even just read-only information, employing industry-standard security practices is paramount for earning and keeping user trust.

A solid foundation often begins with **least-privilege principles**. Instead of requesting broad browser permissions—like reading every website—focus on the few you absolutely need. During one project, I realized I'd set the extension to allow ".*" domain access, even though I only needed a handful of sites. Reducing that scope meant users felt safer, and in turn, I had fewer worries about accidental data leaks. The less you ask from the browser, the less can potentially go wrong.

Securing your **internal and external communications** is another huge step. That means using HTTPS whenever you communicate with a server, verifying certificate trust, and encrypting sensitive details. I once integrated with a chat service that only had HTTP endpoints. My extension was broadcasting user IDs in plain text. Not surprisingly, it led to some user hesitation. I ended up switching to a more secure service, and the difference in user confidence was immediate. The extra friction involved in setting up secure connections is small potatoes compared to the nightmare of compromised data.

Then there's the question of **storing tokens or passwords**. I see a lot of new developers keep them in plain text in either localStorage or even embedded in their scripts. That's a big no-no. While storing tokens in an extension is always a bit risky, you can minimize exposure by using short-lived tokens and implementing refresh mechanisms. I prefer to store them in memory or use secure browser storage that automatically encrypts data. Wherever they land, it's crucial that you don't log them or inadvertently expose them through debugging statements.

Code **integrity checks** are yet another layer of protection. Sometimes, malicious actors manipulate extensions after they're installed, substituting scripts to mine data or run hidden tasks. I mitigate this risk by signing my code with the store's publishing tools, so if any tampering occurs, the extension's signature breaks. Granted, sophisticated hackers can still find ways around such measures, but I always say: the more obstacles you put in their path, the better. Ensuring the code you write is the code users are actually running is half the security battle.

Additionally, it's smart to establish a **response plan** for potential security issues. If a vulnerability does slip through the cracks, you'll want to patch it quickly. Setting up automated alerts if something strange happens—like an unusual number of requests from your extension—can help you detect malicious activity early. Letting your audience know you're proactive about security can transform a potential crisis into an opportunity to show professionalism and genuine concern for your users' welfare.

Finally, periodic **security reviews** are vital. I block off time every so often to comb through my codebase, re-checking permissions, scanning for outdated libraries, and revisiting areas that handle user data. Even when everything seems fine, an extension's environment can change—updates to Edge, new APIs, or shifts in third-party services. By staying current, you head off issues before they morph into large-scale problems. Through consistent practice, security becomes second nature, ensuring your extension stands firmly on trusted ground.

Chapter 18: Localization and Accessibility

I first dipped my toes into localization when my extension unexpectedly gained popularity in regions where English wasn't the primary language. My inbox started filling up with user requests in Spanish, French, and Japanese, asking for translations. It was a bit of a wake-up call. While the underlying functionality of my extension needed no changes, the user interface wasn't friendly to global audiences. Embracing localization and accessibility transformed my project from a niche tool into something that users worldwide could genuinely feel was made just for them.

Localization generally starts with **string externalization**. Instead of hard-coding text, I store every piece of user-facing text in resource files. The beauty of Microsoft Edge is that it provides special support for localized extensions, like the **_locales** folder. Each subfolder within it corresponds to a different language, and I simply translate my strings in the corresponding JSON files. Doing this felt cumbersome at first—I had to label every label, tooltip, and error message. But once you lay the groundwork, adding a new language is just a matter of dropping in another set of translations.

A major revelation for me was the **cultural nuances** in language. For instance, certain idioms or phrases don't for many other users who rely on shortcuts or alternative browsing methods.

When implementing both localization and accessibility, **documentation** plays a helpful role. I keep a chart of the languages I'm supporting, along with each translator's contact information or at least a link to reference material. For accessibility, I document what guidelines I've followed—such as WCAG 2.1 compliance—and maintain checklists of tasks like verifying color contrast and testing with screen readers. Having these references streamlined my development cycle significantly.

In wrapping my head around globalization, I realized it was less about checking boxes and more about opening doors. Localization invites people from different linguistic backgrounds to engage with your extension. Accessibility, on the other hand, welcomes those who navigate the online world in nontraditional ways. Each improvement fosters a deeper sense of community. I've seen how inclusivity can lift a project to new heights, broadening your user base and cultivating loyalty from individuals who feel seen and accommodated. Ultimately, forging a path toward worldwide usability isn't just good ethics—it's good business.

Chapter 19: Cross-Browser Compatibility

Early in my journey, I happily built my extension for Microsoft Edge and assumed that would be enough. Then I noticed a wave of users wondering if the same extension could run on Chrome, Firefox, or other browsers. At first, the idea of juggling multiple platforms seemed overwhelming. Could I really maintain several codebases? But I soon discovered that Edge's Chromium foundation and the growing alignment of browser APIs made cross-browser compatibility way less painful than I'd imagined. In fact, it became an intriguing puzzle—how do I adapt one extension so it fits neatly into various browser ecosystems?

The first tip is to **leverage universal web standards** as much as possible. If your extension uses standard JavaScript, CSS, and HTML, you're already better positioned for cross-browser success. When I started mixing in exotic features that only Edge supported, I had to come up with fallback solutions or polyfills to mimic similar functionality in other browsers. For instance, if one API didn't exist in Firefox, I'd either find an alternative solution or gracefully disable that feature in the Firefox build. Being mindful of these differences from the outset can save you a lot of retrofitting later.

Though Edge, Chrome, and Opera share the Chromium engine, minor **manifest variations** still exist. I typically keep a single manifest file but conditionally include or exclude specific permissions or fields at build time. Some developers automate this with build scripts that generate a fresh manifest for each target browser. Another approach is to keep separate manifest files—one for Edge, one for Chrome, and so on—though I find that method can create extra overhead when it's time to make updates.

Firefox, on the other hand, follows a slightly different path with **WebExtensions**. It does share many of the same APIs as Chromium-based browsers, but you might bump into some subtle differences. I recall one project where the background script's messaging mechanism in Firefox required me to rename certain event listeners. The good news is these changes are usually small. Mozilla's developer documentation often provides a direct mapping between Chrome APIs and their Firefox equivalents, saving me hours of guesswork.

Once you've addressed the code differences, **testing** becomes your best friend. I keep multiple browser environments handy—Edge, Chrome, Firefox, and sometimes even Brave. I walk through my extension's core features in each browser, looking for quirks or unexpected behaviors. Does the popup scale correctly? Do content scripts load on the intended websites with the proper permissions? If you find issues, a debug console in each browser will typically point you toward the culprit. It's an iterative process, but it pays off once you see your extension humming along smoothly across different platforms.

Deployment is another juggling act. Each browser has its own store—Chrome Web Store, Firefox Add-ons, Opera Add-ons—and typically requires a slightly different submission process or packaging method. I've learned to maintain a simple checklist: update version numbers, re-check manifest fields, re-test critical features, and compile the final zip file. This approach helps avoid silly mistakes like forgetting to enable or disable a certain permission for a specific store.

In hindsight, expanding to multiple browsers elevated my extension's reach and sharpened my coding skills. It's exhilarating to know that someone using Firefox on a Linux machine can enjoy the same benefits as someone on Windows Edge. While each new platform introduces its own hoops and hurdles, the broad exposure, user feedback, and recognition you gain feel incredibly rewarding. For me, cross-browser compatibility symbolizes adaptability. It's about making your extension accessible to as many people as possible—regardless of their browsing preferences—and in the process, boosting your reputation as a developer who delivers consistent, high-quality experiences wherever users roam.

Chapter 20: Gathering and Analyzing User Feedback

I still remember the first time I discovered how transformative user feedback could be for my extension. After launching a basic prototype, I started receiving messages from a handful of folks who expressed genuine excitement about what I'd built. At the same time, I got critical comments calling out incomplete features or confusing interfaces, which made me cringe initially. But as uncomfortable as it felt, those messages revealed blind spots and inspired me to refine everything from my design to the underlying logic.

Gathering feedback begins with making your users feel welcome to share their thoughts. I tried everything—I added a link to a "Send Feedback" form right in my extension's popup, sprinkled an invitation on my landing page, and even mentioned it in my changelog. It never fails to surprise me how often people are willing to share their impressions if you simply show that you're open to hearing them. Some of the most obvious user experience problems I've fixed were brought to my attention through a few lines of user text.

Still, not all feedback is equal. Early on, I treated every suggestion like it was top priority. That approach nearly buried me in half-finished experiments. Over time, I learned to categorize comments. For instance, if several users repeatedly mentioned the need for a dark mode, I'd elevate that request to a must-have. On the other hand, a one-off request for a niche feature might go on the back burner. This method allowed me to be responsive while avoiding feature creep, which can dilute the core purpose of the extension.

To make sense of broader patterns, I started using simple analytics—like how many times the extension's popup was opened daily, which features were clicked most, or how often errors showed up in the logs. These metrics served as a crucial context for my user feedback. If someone said a feature was too hard to find, I could check whether the usage metrics aligned with their complaint. It was fascinating to watch real data confirm some suspicions and disprove others.

Of course, numbers alone don't paint the full picture. I discovered that context matters. One user might be a power user who's pushing the extension to its limits, while another might just be getting acquainted with browser tools. Sometimes, a problem that vexes an experienced developer barely registers with a casual user, and vice versa. I learned to pay close attention to who was giving the feedback and what their use case resembled.

I also realized it helps to go where your users congregate. If you have a social media group or a dedicated forum, that's probably where you'll see more candid discussions. People might share tips on using your extension in ways you never intended, or collectively gripe about a bug they all encounter. These unfiltered chatters can be gold, because often, users will offer their own solutions. In one instance, I found a lengthy thread of advanced tips created by enthusiasts who'd discovered clever workarounds for my extension's limits.

When it comes to actually analyzing feedback, I use a combination of intuition and structure. I'll tally comments about design issues, code improvements, or performance complaints in a spreadsheet. Then I weigh which changes bring the most benefit to the largest number of people. Over time, I discovered that even negative feedback contains seeds of positivity because it sparks new ideas. If you maintain an open mind— staying curious rather than defensive—that's when your extension truly evolves.

It's an ongoing cycle: gather feedback, analyze the patterns, make informed improvements, then gather fresh feedback to assess the results. With each iteration, I've watched my extension blossom away from my original assumptions toward something that genuinely resonates with my audience. In the end, user feedback isn't just commentary; it's a dynamic blueprint guiding every stage of your extension's growth. Embracing it wholeheartedly can be the difference between a project that languishes and one that continually thrives.

translate neatly, or a date format that makes sense in North America might confuse users in Europe. My approach is to rely on professional translators or at least native speakers to refine my text, especially in languages I'm unfamiliar with. If the extension is more technical, sometimes a direct translation works, but for a mainstream audience, a culturally tuned approach goes a long way in showing respect and attention to detail.

Parallel to localization is the realm of **accessibility**. I learned about how important accessible design was when a user reached out, explaining that their visual impairment prevented them from effectively seeing my extension's interface. That sparked a deep dive into best practices. First on the docket was ensuring I used correct semantic markup. For example, employing *aria-label* tags so screen readers can interpret buttons properly. I also made sure color contrasts met recommended guidelines. It's easy to pick a color scheme that looks stylish but fails to meet the text contrast requirements for visually impaired users.

Another step involved testing with tools like screen readers. I had a friend who navigates the web using only keyboard input and voice commands. Watching them test my extension was eye-opening. Tiny design issues I'd never noticed—like a tab order that didn't match the visual layout—were glaring obstacles in their workflow. By adding clear focus states, consistent keyboard navigation, and properly labeled elements, I not only helped them but also improved the experience

Chapter 21: Iterating Through Updates

I've often joked that an extension is never truly "done"—it just keeps evolving in the wild. After all, once user feedback rolls in and fresh ideas come to light, you realize there's always more to refine. This iterative process can feel exhilarating, especially when you watch your extension morph from its initial vision into a polished, feature-rich tool. However, it's also easy to get lost in constant tweaking. Striking a balance between rapid experimentation and responsible releases became one of my biggest challenges.

The first step in any iteration is identifying why you're updating. Perhaps you've found a bug that users can't tolerate any longer, or maybe you've decided to introduce a much-requested feature. Sometimes, an iteration revolves around design enhancements—like reorganizing the user interface for clarity. As long as you set a clear objective before diving in, you're far less likely to introduce random changes that bloat the extension or confuse your user base.

I learned early on that **version control** is a developer's best friend. By branching off a stable version and experimenting on a separate branch, I preserved a reliable fallback in case my new ideas went haywire. This setup also allowed me to test multiple updates simultaneously, merging them only when I felt confident about their stability. It's a safety net that has saved me from disastrous rollbacks more times than I can count.

Once the coding part of an update is finished, I shift into a **preview phase**. This is where I distribute a beta version of the extension to a small circle of testers—often a combination of curious friends and power users who enjoy exclusive previews. Their feedback is invaluable because it catches flaws I might be too close to see. By the time I release those updates publicly, I'm typically more confident in my changes. Plus, offering a sneak peek can make your beta testers feel invested in the extension's success.

Another lesson I've learned is to communicate changes clearly. Whenever I introduce a new feature, I note it in the release logs, alongside a brief explanation of how to use it. If I remove or alter an existing feature, I explain why, so users aren't left scratching their heads. This transparency fosters trust and eases the transition for people who might otherwise feel blindsided by big modifications. In my experience, a short paragraph in the release notes can prevent a torrent of confused emails later.

Of course, each iteration brings the risk of **new bugs**. Even if you meticulously test, some elusive glitch may slip through. That's why I always keep an eye on crash reports, error logs, and user submissions after rollout. Sometimes, a simple patch can fix an oversight, but only if I'm alert enough to catch it quickly. Check in daily or weekly, depending on how active your user base is, to ensure nothing catastrophic arises from your well-intentioned improvements.

The final aspect of iteration involves analyzing the results. Did the new feature spike usage? Are fewer people reporting confusion about the interface? Have performance stats improved? By comparing these metrics to your goals, you can gauge whether to keep iterating on a particular feature or pivot to a different priority. If you're anything like me, you'll find genuine excitement in this cycle. There's a sense of progress every time you refine your extension in direct response to real-world needs.

Ultimately, maintaining an iterative mindset means embracing change as a core part of the extension's lifecycle. It keeps your project fresh, relevant, and aligned with evolving browser standards. More importantly, it lets your audience know you're committed to delivering the best possible experience. By continually refining and updating, you earn a reputation for reliability and innovation, which sets your extension apart from the sea of alternatives on the market.

Chapter 22: Building an Engaged User Community

I'll never forget the day my email inbox was flooded with supportive messages from users who had discovered each other on social media and started discussing my extension's features at length. It was an incredible moment—a spark that began forming a real community around the work I'd poured so much energy into. From that day forward, I realized that the best extension communities don't just happen; they need to be nurtured, guided, and celebrated to thrive.

One of my first steps was creating a central gathering space—be it a Facebook group, a subforum on my website, or a dedicated Discord channel—where users could share tips, feedback, and success stories. This was a game-changer. Suddenly, people who had been using the extension in isolation found a place to connect, trade advice, and even troubleshoot one another's questions. In this environment, I witnessed the birth of mini-experts who knew certain extension features better than even I did.

Encouraging user-led discussions in these groups turned out to be a major advantage. Occasionally, a user would have a tricky question, but before I could respond, another community member would jump in with the perfect solution. This kind of peer-to-peer support not only saved me time, it also made the extension feel like a collective project. People love to share knowledge, and a supportive community can ignite a cycle of paying it forward.

While user-driven conversations are valuable, I also believe in organized events or challenges. For instance, if your extension helps with productivity, you could host a monthly challenge where community members share their best workflow hacks. I've seen participants bond over their creative uses of my tool, forging friendships and raising each other's skill levels. Structured events keep the community vibrant and give people fresh reasons to check in regularly.

On the developer's side, transparency and accessibility deepen community trust. If users sense that I'm present, ready to answer queries or gather suggestions, they feel more invested. I set aside specific windows when I'm available for live Q&A sessions or quick how-to tutorials. These real-time interactions make me more than just a name on the extension's listing; they humanize the entire project and let people see that there's an actual person behind the code.

Moderation is vital, too. While I aim to keep discussions open-ended, spam and inflammatory remarks can derail an otherwise positive space. I designate a few community members as volunteer moderators and draft concise rules that focus on respect and constructiveness. This gentle framework ensures that new users feel safe to ask questions without fear of ridicule. A pleasant, orderly environment fosters deeper connections and encourages lurkers to step out and engage.

Over time, I've learned that highlighting user contributions strengthens the sense of belonging. When someone uncovers a hidden trick or puts together a valuable tutorial, I'll spotlight it in a newsletter or on social media. This not only rewards the contributor with a bit of recognition, but also motivates others to share their discoveries. Recognition can come in various forms: a simple shout-out, a badge system, or a small perk in your extension itself, like early access to new features.

Ultimately, an engaged user community can lift your extension to heights you'd never reach alone. It becomes a living, breathing entity that evolves with the shared experiences of everyone involved. People form genuine friendships, trade knowledge, and lend support, all driven by their enthusiasm for what you've created. And in those moments—watching your community thrive—you realize you haven't just built an extension. You've built a fellowship, bound by a shared passion to make browsing better for everyone.

Chapter 23: Embracing Innovation and Emerging Trends

I still recall the day someone asked me if my extension supported a voice-control feature. It was an idea that had never crossed my mind, yet it perfectly captured the spirit of staying ahead of the curve. As technology evolves at breakneck speed, browsers keep rolling out new APIs, and user expectations shift. If you want your extension to remain relevant, you can't just settle for your current success. You need to keep your eyes peeled for fresh opportunities and be prepared to embrace the unexpected.

One of the ways I stay abreast of emerging trends is by following official announcements and developer blogs from browser vendors. They often tease upcoming APIs or highlight shifts in design philosophy. When I read about progressive enhancements—like the introduction of the File System Access API—I start brainstorming how it might unlock a new angle for my extension. Sometimes, these explorations lead to implementing optional features that set my tool apart, drawing curious new users who crave the latest functionality.

Similarly, I've learned to keep an eye on user behavior changes. As more people start browsing the web from mobile devices or connecting multiple devices in a single account, I realized my extension would benefit from seamless syncing and responsive interfaces. Initially, I dismissed these ideas as out of scope. But once I saw how many users were juggling tabs on tablets and phones, I recognized the need to pivot. Introducing cross-device syncing wasn't just a bonus; it quickly became a defining reason why people chose my extension over others.

Another powerful tactic is studying what's happening offline, not just online. I've drawn inspiration from assistant-based apps, VR/AR tools, and even robotics. While those fields might seem unrelated, they often introduce new paradigms that can trickle down to web technologies. For instance, voice recognition technology used in smart speakers eventually found its way into browser extensions, enabling voice-activated commands. By staying curious and willing to adapt, I've managed to incorporate out-of-the-box features that surprise users in a delightful way.

Collaboration with other developers or service providers can also spark innovation. I recall partnering with a machine learning startup that specialized in text analysis. By integrating their neural engine, I took my extension's text-reading capability to a whole new level, automatically summarizing articles for busy users. That leap in innovation drew rave reviews from people who were always on the go, showcasing just how impactful a well-chosen collaboration can be.

Of course, you won't implement every new technology that comes along. I learned the hard way that chasing shiny objects without careful consideration can lead to half-finished experiments and user confusion. Instead, I practice a method of prototyping small, time-bound projects to test feasibility. If initial tests show promise, I commit more resources. If they flop or feel too forced, I shelve them for later. This approach keeps me nimble without derailing my extension's core mission.

There's also a philosophical aspect to embracing innovation. If you cling too tightly to how things "should be," you risk fossilizing your extension. My motto became: keep an open mind, but maintain a clear sense of purpose. Some of my most innovative features came from asking, "What if?" then following that thread just far enough to see if it blossomed into something genuinely useful. This spirit of exploration has kept me excited about my work, even when the to-do list grows lengthy.

Ultimately, integrating new technology and trends goes beyond shiny marketing points. It shows your users you're invested in delivering cutting-edge value. As more industries blur lines—like machine learning, voice control, and extended reality—browser extensions can evolve to meet those frontiers. Yes, it requires effort, imagination, and sometimes a willingness to fail. But in the end, those leaps keep your extension vibrant, relevant, and endlessly captivating in a world that's always looking for the next big thing.

Chapter 24: Scaling Your Extension Business

The first time I realized my extension had outgrown its modest beginnings, I felt equal parts excitement and trepidation. On one hand, I was thrilled that something I created could have real business potential, reaching more people than I ever imagined. On the other, I worried whether I had the skills, infrastructure, or strategy to handle this new scale. Over time, I learned that growing an extension from a tiny side project to a serious enterprise requires more than just adding features—it demands a thoughtful approach to expansion in every aspect of the business.

A core component of scaling is **optimizing your operations**. In the early days, I would manually respond to support emails and process payments. That worked when I had maybe ten messages a week. But as my user base soared into the thousands, I had to begin automating. I integrated help desk software to funnel inquiries into tickets, assigned them priority levels, and set up automated responses for common questions. This smaller shift saved me hours each day, allowing me to focus on complex issues and strategic growth.

Monetization strategies also evolve as you scale. I found that while donations or minimal ads might suffice initially, higher revenue goals call for stable income streams. For instance, when I introduced premium subscription tiers, I had to think about secure payment gateways, user management systems, and even the possibility of annual billing discounts. Suddenly, my extension wasn't just a tool, but a bona fide SaaS (Software as a Service) product. Users expected professional support, reliable uptime, and ongoing improvements—obligations that swelled alongside my growing revenue.

With more users comes the need to **fortify your infrastructure**. If your extension relies on external servers—like storing user data or running computational tasks—those servers need to handle surges in traffic. For me, that meant moving from a shared hosting setup to a scalable cloud platform. Yes, it meant shifting to a slightly higher operating cost, but the payoff was peace of mind. Whenever unexpected spikes occurred—maybe after a positive review on a popular tech blog—my system could pivot quickly.

Another tip: consider enlisting **help**. In the beginning, I was a one-person show—coding, designing, marketing, and troubleshooting. While that's a great way to learn, it's not sustainable once your user base balloons. Whether it's collaborating with a freelance designer for branding refreshes or bringing on a dedicated marketer, extra hands let you maintain consistent quality. For me, hiring a part-time customer support person was revolutionary. Users got faster replies, and I freed mental space to address bigger development challenges.

Scaling also calls for a **long-term roadmap**. Initially, my updates were more impulsive: I'd fix a bug here, add a small feature there whenever time allowed. But with a growing audience, people began to depend on these updates and plan their usage around new releases. That meant establishing a release cycle—maybe monthly or quarterly—and announcing upcoming improvements so users could anticipate the changes. This shift improved predictability and eased the burden on my support team, as we all knew what was coming down the pipeline.

However, expansion doesn't always go smoothly. I've hit snags where new features introduced unexpected performance issues, or a server upgrade temporarily locked out some international users. Instead of seeing these moments as disasters, I embraced them as learning experiences. Apologizing transparently, explaining the cause, and describing the steps to prevent a repeat often turned frustrated users into some of my biggest supporters. Openness in times of crisis can deepen trust more than smooth sailing ever could.

Reflecting on this journey, I realize how "scaling" is more than a buzzword—it's a fundamental shift in perspective. You're no longer building a neat personal project; you're stewarding a platform or service that can empower countless people. This means stepping up to new responsibilities: stable infrastructure, reliable support, polished updates, and possibly a growing team. Each step can be daunting, but with consistent effort and a willingness to adapt, scaling your extension business becomes the logical next stage in transforming a promising idea into a thriving, impactful enterprise.

Chapter 25: Success Stories and Future Outlook

I'll never forget the flash of excitement I felt when I first started spotting user reviews praising my extension's practicality and ease of use. Before I knew it, my inbox overflowed with heartfelt success stories—people who'd used my browser tool to streamline their workloads, organize their daily tasks, or even launch entire projects of their own. Those messages validated my belief that a well-designed Microsoft Edge extension could become so much more than a simple add-on; it could spark changes, push new ideas into the spotlight, and end up shaping someone's online experience in powerful ways.

One story that stands out involves a fellow developer who created an Edge extension to track local farmers' markets. Their goal was modest: list what produce was in season and show where users could find the freshest deals. Over time, the extension morphed into a small hub for farm-to-table enthusiasts, even featuring weekly recipe ideas based on what's currently available. The real kicker? Local growers began seeing increased foot traffic, and word spread like wildfire on social media. Sales shot up during harvest season. Before long, the developer found themselves partnering with local businesses to offer exclusive deals to extension users. That's the beauty of starting small and gradually expanding—sometimes, all you need is that first nudge to transform an idea into something that truly impacts your community.

Another personal favorite involves a team of educators who designed an extension to help students keep track of online resources. The group had initially intended it as a simple bookmark manager with a rating feature—students could rate sites based on relevance and clarity. But as word spread around campus, the extension evolved into a collaborative platform. Different colleges adopted it for various subjects, from English Literature to Computer Science, enabling entire classes to vote on the most helpful articles and videos. The educators confided to me that they'd never seen such engagement from their students before. The extension encouraged a sense of ownership over the learning process—an experience that truly encapsulated how software can drive community-building.

Then there's the solo entrepreneur who devised a translation extension aimed at small e-commerce merchants. She integrated third-party APIs to handle everything from currency conversions to localized product descriptions. At first, she relied on a freemium model, but the tool's accuracy and speed led to a flurry of upgrades. Soon, her extension became indispensable for international sellers trying to bridge linguistic gaps. Over the past year, she's scaled her server capacity several times to match demand. In her emails to me, she wrote how it felt surreal to watch a side project evolve into a real business, netting enough income to cover her living expenses and then some.

Stories like these highlight a common thread: with the right blend of vision, execution, and user feedback, a Microsoft Edge extension can explode into unforeseen realms of success. I've observed that most of these success narratives share a few key elements. First, they address a tangible need—usually something the community has been clamoring for. Second, they grow by listening to users. That constant collaboration weaves a sense of shared ownership and keeps momentum high. Finally, these creators remain curious, adapting to shifting market trends and adopting new technologies without losing sight of their extension's core purpose.

Looking ahead, it's clear that the future of Edge extensions continues to evolve. As the browser integrates more with emerging fields—like artificial intelligence, virtual and augmented reality, and robust cloud infrastructures—extensions will become increasingly powerful. We might see voice-activated plugins that handle entire sequences of web interactions, or real-time translation systems that adapt the text on any page into a preferred dialect. For developers, the big opportunity lies in staying agile: when a promising API appears, be ready to experiment.

Furthermore, collaboration between extensions might usher in a new wave of user experiences. Imagine if your note-taking add-on easily synced content to your personal finance tool, highlighting budget-friendly shopping lists. Or your language-learning extension could seamlessly pair with an AI writing assistant for real-time grammar checks. The possibilities spin out faster than we can name them, but each new idea symbolizes fresh ground for developers to cover.

In many ways, success stories and an optimistic outlook go hand in hand. The more we celebrate breakthroughs, the more we're reminded that each extension can spark its own ripple effect. Every time a single user's life gets a bit easier, every time a small business sees measurable growth, or every time a classroom unites around a creative learning tool, the extension ecosystem becomes richer. And that's perhaps the greatest motivator of all: this world of possibilities isn't shrinking—it's expanding, making room for anyone ready to dream big and follow through.

www.ingramcontent.com/pod-product-compliance
Lightning Source LLC
LaVergne TN
LVHW051747050326
832903LV00029B/2777